MOTHS

Jen Green

Grolier
an imprint of

www.scholastic.com/librarypublishing

Published 2008 by Grolier
An imprint of Scholastic Library Publishing
Old Sherman Turnpike, Danbury,
Connecticut 06816

For The Brown Reference Group plc
Project Editor: Jolyon Goddard
Copy-editors: Ann Baggaley, Tom Jackson
Picture Researcher: Clare Newman
Designers: Jeni Child, Lynne Ross,
Sarah Williams
Managing Editor: Bridget Giles

Volume ISBN-13: 978-0-7172-6271-7
Volume ISBN-10: 0-7172-6271-5

Library of Congress Cataloging-in-Publication Data

Nature's children. Set 3.
p. cm.
Includes bibliographical references and index.
ISBN 13: 978-0-7172-8082-7
ISBN 10: 0-7172-8082-9
1. Animals--Encyclopedias, Juvenile. I. Grolier Educational (Firm)
QL49.N384 2008
590.3--dc22
2007031568

Printed and bound in China

PICTURE CREDITS

Front Cover: **NHPA**: Robert Thompson.

Back Cover: **Nature PL**: Hans Christoph Kappel; **Shutterstock**: Lee and Marleigh Freyenhagen, Geoffrey Kuchera, Alexander Makismenko.

FLPA: Mitsuhiko Inamori 17, Norbert Wu 29; **Nature PL**: Ingo Arndt 38, 42, Jane Burton 46, De Cuveland/Arco 41, Hanne and Jens Eriksen 14, Ross Hoddinott 30, Hans Christoph Kappel 34, Kim Taylor 9, Doug Wechsler 6; **Shutterstock**: Anyka 10, EcoPrint, 4, 18, Daniel Kelly 5, Cheryl Kunde 45, Bruce MacQueen 21, Alexander Makismenko 22, Perrush 2–3, Floris Slooff 26–27, Jens Stolt 37, **Still Pictures**: Matt Meadows 33, Tom Vezo 13.

Contents

Fact File: Moths 4
Scaly Wings 7
Moth or Butterfly? 8
Shapes and Sizes 11
Moth Country 12
Skillful Fliers 15
Attracted to Light 16
Sensing the World 19
Super Sight 20
Sipping Nectar 23
Helping Plants 24
In Disguise 25
Feature Photo 26–27
Fooling Enemies 28
Time to Breed 31
Starting Life 32
Hatching Out 35
Born to Eat 36

A New Suit 39

Staying Alive 40

Ready for Change 43

Transformation 44

Friend or Foe? 47

Spotting Moths 48

Words to Know 49

Find Out More 51

Index 52

FACT FILE: Moths

Class	Insects (Insecta)
Order	Moths and butterflies (Lepidoptera)
Families	About 100 families
Genera	Hundreds of genera
Species	More than 150,000 species
World distribution	Moths live in all parts of the world except the coldest places at the top of high mountains or in the polar regions; moths are most common in the warm tropics
Habitat	Many places, including fields and woods
Distinctive physical characteristics	These insects are very similar to butterflies, but they often have less colorful wings and a furrier body; the antennas, or feelers, are feathery or threadlike
Habits	Most moths fly at night and are attracted to light; young undergo complete metamorphosis before becoming adults
Diet	Varies with species; caterpillars usually eat plant food of some kind

Introduction

Many people think of moths as drab cousins of butterflies. However, some moths are just as bright and colorful as butterflies. Even moths that look dull at first glance often have beautiful patterns once you take a closer look.

Whatever their color, moths are amazing creatures. They have highly developed senses and clever ways of foiling their enemies. The moth's life cycle, in which a tiny egg grows into a **caterpillar**, which in turn changes into a winged adult, is one of the most incredible stories in nature.

Moths lie their wings flat when resting.

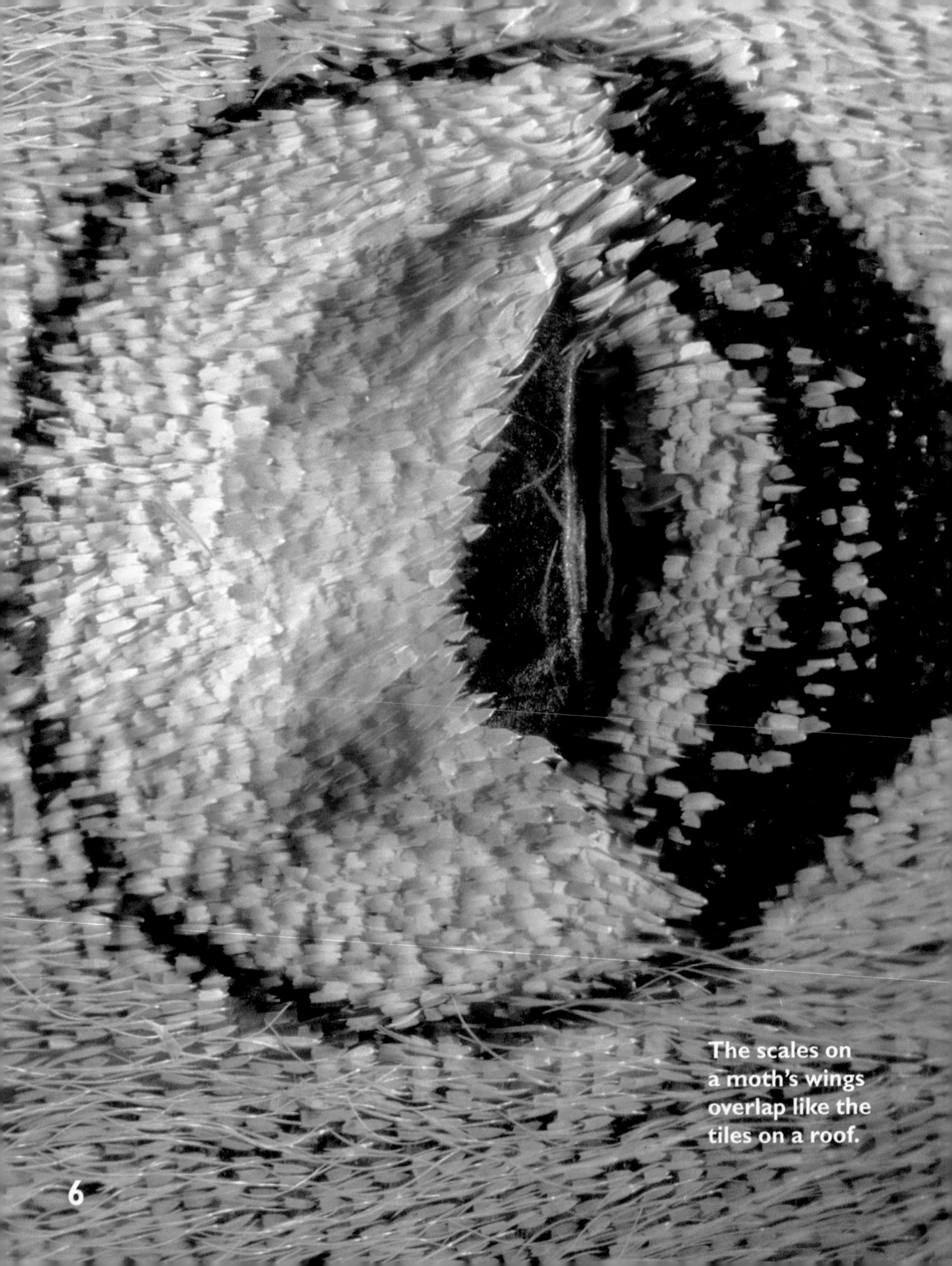

The scales on
a moth's wings
overlap like the
tiles on a roof.

Scaly Wings

Moths are a type of insect. The insect world is huge, with many millions of **species**. Scientists divide this vast set of animals into groups called orders. Each order contains several families of insects. One of the insect orders contains all the moths and butterflies.

The name of the moth and butterfly order is Lepidoptera. That is a Greek word meaning "scale-wings." The surface of a moth's wings is covered with tiny scales. These rub off as a fine dust if you touch them. The scales give the moth's wings their color and also help to protect the insect from harm.

Moth or Butterfly?

Moths and butterflies can look very similar. It is not always easy to tell one from the other. However, there are some differences between the two insects.

Moths have a furrier, thicker body than butterflies. Moths usually fly during the night while butterflies are most active in daylight. Moths usually rest with their wings open wide. Butterflies shut their wings and hold them upright when they land.

Moths and butterflies both have **antennas**, or feelers. While the antennas of butterflies have tiny blobs on the tips, a moth's antennas are fine threads or branched and feathery.

Unlike butterflies, moths fly in the dark so they are not interested in colorful blooms.

The moth's front and back wings are hooked together so they work like a single large wing.

Shapes and Sizes

Moths far outnumber their better-known relatives. There are around 15,000 species, or types, of butterflies, but there are more than ten times as many moth species.

Moths come in many different shapes, sizes, and colors. The largest measure a whopping 10 inches (25 cm) across. The smallest are so tiny that they are almost impossible to see. Whatever their size, all moths share the same basic body structure. Like other insects, the moth's body is divided into three sections—the head, **thorax**, or middle part, and abdomen, or rear section. All moths have two pairs of wings.

Moth Country

Moths look delicate, but they are surprisingly tough. Moths are able to survive in most places, including forests, woodlands, and grasslands. Some live in mountain meadows or on the treeless tundra in the far north. Other moths make their home in deserts. In fact, there are very few places on Earth where moths do not live.

In North America alone there may be about 15,000 different types of moths. No one knows the exact number of species. It is always going up, as new types of moths are discovered regularly. Scientists know a lot less about moths than butterflies. That is because moths are active at night when it is more difficult to study their behavior.

A moth's dull
colors allow it
to stay out of sight
in most places.

Hawk moths have triangular-shaped wings like a jet fighter. The shape allows them to fly quickly and make sharp turns in the air.

Skillful Fliers

Moths are expert fliers, among the best of the insects. The two pairs of wings are attached to the thorax—the central body section. The front and hind wings overlap to form a single surface that pushes against the air.

Hawk moths are the fastest moths. They fly at up to 37 miles (60 km) per hour. Hawk moths can also hover in front of flowers like hummingbirds.

Some moths fly on long, annual journeys called migrations. They spend the winter in the warmer regions before flying hundreds of miles north in spring. Once the moths have returned to their northern homes, they lay their eggs. For example, the oleander hawk moth spends winter in Africa and then heads all the way to Europe to breed.

Attracted to Light

Moths are famous for being nocturnal, or active at night. Moths are also known for being attracted to light. If the light in question is a flame or hot lamp, the moth can hurt itself. The common phrase, “like a moth to a flame” is used to describe a person who is attracted to something that will harm him or her.

So why are moths attracted to light? Nobody is sure. One theory is that moths find their way using the light of the Moon. As they fly along, the moths make sure that the Moon is always in the same place—on their left or right. However, moths mistake streetlights for the Moon. As they try to keep the lights in the same place, the moths get confused and flutter around and around in circles.

Scientist use lights to attract moths. They collect the insects to look for new species.

A moth's feathery antennas collect odor particles from the air.

Sensing the World

Moths sense the world using sight, smell, hearing, taste, and touch. Though humans use these senses, too, a moth's senses work in a very different way. The most important sense organs are the two antennas on top of the insect's head. Those are used as feelers, but they are also sensitive to smell and sometimes even taste. The moth's powerful sense of smell helps it to find food and also locate a **mate** when it is time to breed.

Some of the moth's other sense organs are located in places that might seem strange. The taste organs are located not in the mouth, but on the soles of a moth's feet! That allows the moth to taste what it is walking on. The moth's eardrums are located on its thorax.

Super Sight

A moth's view of the world is very different from that of a human's. Like most other insects, moths have not one, but two types of eyes. Tiny, beadlike eyes, called simple eyes, are located between the antennas. These eyes sense light and dark, but cannot see shapes.

The main set of eyes are the large, round compound eyes. These eyes are made up of many tiny lenses. Scientists believe that each lens sees one small part of the moth's surroundings. Together, the tiny images form a big picture.

Like most people, moths see in color. They can also see ultraviolet light, a type of light that is invisible to humans. Many flowers have patterns that show up in ultraviolet light. Those patterns become obvious to moths in the dim light of dusk.

A moth's compound eyes are very good at sensing movement.

A hawk moth extends its proboscis into a flower while hovering.

Sipping Nectar

Most adult moths feed on liquid plant foods such as fruit juice, sap, and the sugary **nectar** made by flowers. Flowers advertise this food to moths by giving off sweet scents, which the insects pick up with their antennas.

The moth feeds on sugary liquids using long, tube-shaped mouthparts. This slender tube is called a **proboscis**, and it is used like a drinking straw. A moth's proboscis can be as long as the insect itself! When not in use, the moth coils its proboscis under its head. When the moth wants to feed, it lands on a flower. The taste buds on its feet lead it to the nectar at the center of the flower. The moth then uncoils its proboscis and begins to drink.

Helping Plants

Why do plants attract moths with scents and bright patterns and then supply free food to them? The plants need the insects' help. Moths and other insects help plants to breed and make seeds. For a plant's seeds to develop, it needs **pollen**, often from another plant. Moths help plants by transferring pollen from one flower to another.

When the moth visits a flower to feed on nectar, some of the flower's pollen rubs off on the insect. When the moth moves to the next flower, the pollen falls off and is collected by the second plant. Moths and butterflies help gardeners and farmers by performing this vital role, which allows plants to grow back year after year.

In Disguise

Some moths are just as brightly colored as butterflies. For example, the great tiger moth has bold yellow, brown, and black markings—like a tiger. However, many moths have less obvious coloring. These drab patterns and colors let the moths blend in with their surroundings. The peppered moth looks just like tree bark. This coloring, called **camouflage**, makes it very hard for enemies to see the moth.

Underwing moths have the best of both worlds—they are both drab and brightly colored! They have dull-colored front wings and bright red or yellow hind wings. That allows them to do an amazing vanishing trick. An enemy chasing the fluttering moth focuses on its colorful hind wings. When the moth lands, it hides the hind wings under the camouflaged forewings. Without the bright wings to follow, the hunter can no longer see the moth.

Atlas moths are among the largest moths in the world. Their wingspan can reach 10 inches (25 cm).

Fooling Enemies

Moths are hunted by many **predators**, including bats, cats, and birds. Fortunately for moths, they have some clever ways of escaping these enemies.

Io (I-OH) moths have two large, dark markings on their wings, that look like huge eyes. When the moth spreads its wings, the two large "eyes" appear. For a moment, a predator is fooled into thinking it is face to face with a large and dangerous animal, such as an owl. As the hunter hesitates, the moth flutters away.

Tiger moths use another trick to escape bats, which hunt at night. Bats produce a stream of clicking sounds and then listen out for echoes that bounce off moths or other insects. That is how bats track their **prey**. Some tiger moths produce their own clicking sounds. Those confuse the bats, so they cannot find their prey.

Io moths usually keep their eyespots hidden under their forewings.

Burnet moths, such as these two, are active during the day. Their red spots warn predators that they are poisonous.

Time to Breed

Moths do not live for very long. Adult moths spend a lot of their time searching for mates, so they can produce young before they die. Moths time their matings so the young hatch when there is plenty of food for them to eat.

Butterflies attract their mates using bright colors. However, colors are not much use at night. So moths attract their mates using scent instead. Female moths can produce very powerful scents that drift a long way on the wind. The males can pick up the female's scent from several miles away. They follow the scent trail to find the female. Once the male has located the female, the insects mate.

Starting Life

Once the female has mated, she can begin the long process of producing new adult moths. That starts when she lays her eggs. Moth eggs are tiny—no bigger than a pinhead. They may be round or cylinder-shaped. They may be smooth or have ridges. Whatever the shape or texture, they are all camouflaged so they blend in with the leaves, stems, or bark on which they are laid.

The females lay hundreds, sometimes even thousands of eggs. Some females produce eggs in long strings, while others glue them to leaves one by one.

After laying the eggs, the female has nothing more to do with her offspring. She flies off and leaves the eggs to hatch. Most eggs hatch within days or weeks. However, eggs that are laid in late fall do not hatch until the following spring. Then, the weather will be more favorable and there will be plenty of food for the hungry caterpillars.

Female moths lay eggs on something the caterpillars can eat. This promethia moth is laying eggs on a sweet gum plant.

Tiny moth caterpillars break free of their eggs. The first thing they will eat is their egg cases.

Hatching Out

The young insect that hatches from an egg is called a **larva**. A moth larva is more commonly known as a caterpillar. It looks nothing like an adult moth. The caterpillar is wingless, with a long, sausage-shaped body. Some caterpillars have smooth skin while others are bumpy or hairy. In fact, the word caterpillar comes from a French word meaning "hairy cat."

The caterpillar has two antennas to sense its surroundings. It does not have any compound eyes, but has six pairs of simple eyes instead. These eyes do little more than help the caterpillar distinguish light from dark.

The larva has six legs like an adult moth, but there are also up to five pairs of "claspers" or false legs. These are used for walking and gripping. Some moth caterpillars inch along by looping their body into an upside-down U-shape and then straightening out again. Such caterpillars include the inchworm, which is the young of the geometer moth.

Born to Eat

Caterpillars are born hungry. From the moment they hatch they eat more or less constantly. The polyphemus moth caterpillar is the eating champion of the entire animal kingdom. In the first 48 hours of its life it eats 86,000 times its own body weight. That would be like a newborn baby drinking 582,000 pints (273,500 l) of milk!

The caterpillar feeds hungrily on the leaves, stems, wood, or fruit of the plant on which it hatched. Caterpillars have to eat as much as possible. They must grow and gain the energy needed for the next stage of their life.

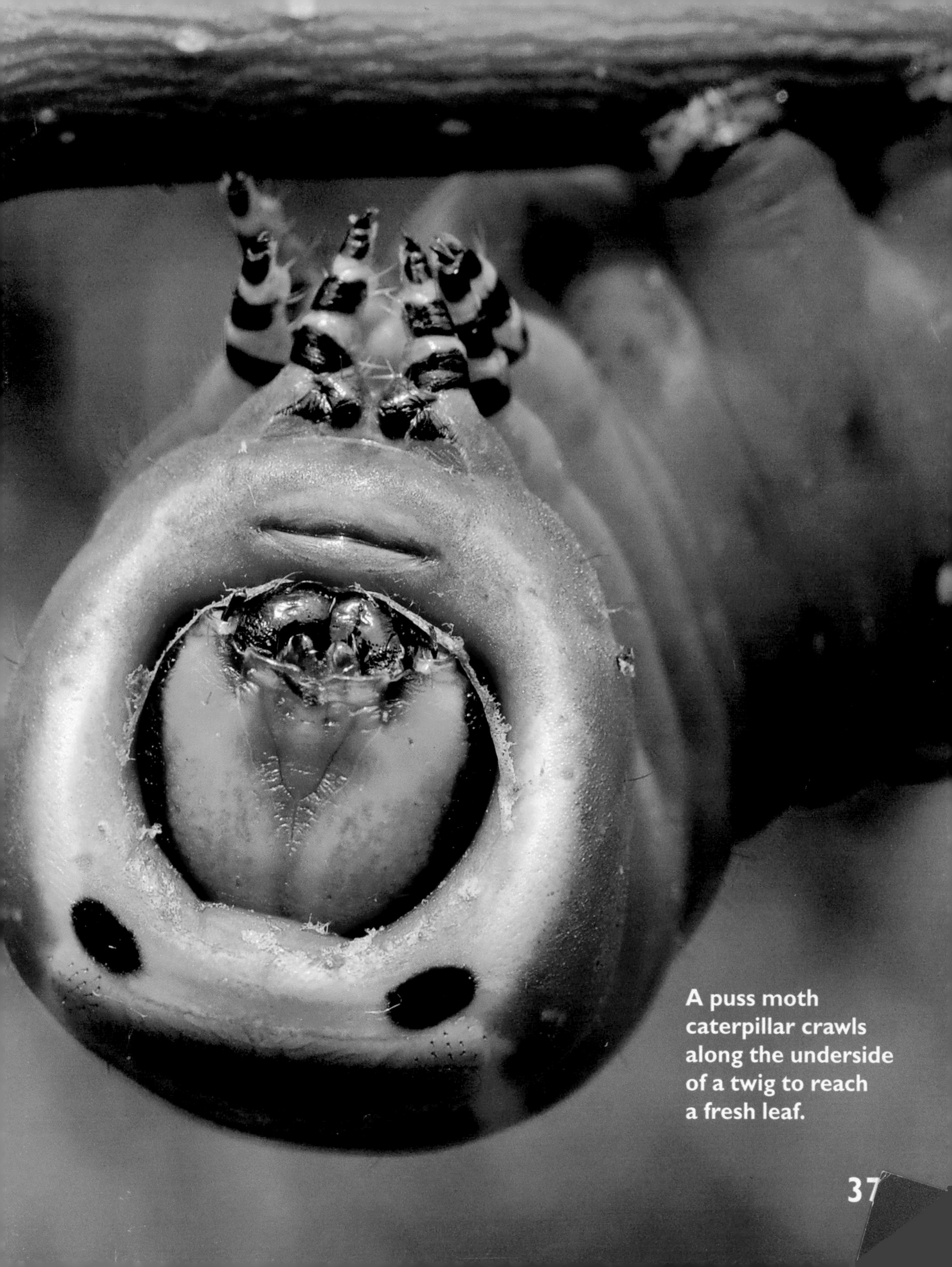

A puss moth caterpillar crawls along the underside of a twig to reach a fresh leaf.

This Atlas moth caterpillar has just molted and has new soft skin. The skin is covered in a wax to protect it until it hardens.

A New Suit

The caterpillar eats night and day, almost without stopping, and grows rapidly. Its skin can stretch as it gets bigger, but not very much. Soon the skin becomes too tight for the caterpillar. The worn-out skin splits along the back, and the caterpillar wriggles out. Fortunately, under the old skin, the caterpillar has a new, looser skin with a bit more space inside for growing. This process is called **molting**, and it happens about five times before the caterpillar is fully grown. After each molt, the first thing many caterpillars do is eat their old skin!

Staying Alive

The world is a dangerous place for moth larvae. Caterpillars make a nourishing meal for frogs, mice, snakes, spiders, birds, and many other animals. Many nesting birds catch about 100 caterpillars every day to feed their young!

Luckily, moth caterpillars have ways of defending themselves against these enemies. Their main defense is to keep hidden. Most caterpillars are green or brown, so they can easily hide among the bark or leaves of trees and shrubs. Some are covered with bristles or spines, which make them hard to eat. Still others are poisonous or taste nasty so their enemies have learned to avoid them.

Caterpillars have another type of enemy that is harder to defend against. Tiny wasps lay their eggs on the caterpillars' backs. When the wasp larvae hatch, they tunnel inside the caterpillar and eat it alive from the inside out!

A sycamore moth caterpillar is covered in fine hairs. The hairs contain chemicals that irritate anything that touches them.

The pupa of a death's head hawk moth is buried in soil. The moth gets its name from the pattern on the adult's back.

Ready for Change

When the caterpillar is fully grown it stops eating and prepares for the next stage in its life cycle. First it finds a sheltered place where it will be safe from predators. Some caterpillars attach themselves to twigs, while others shelter under bark or burrow into the soil.

When the caterpillar molts for the final time it forms a strange, hard-cased object called a **pupa** around itself. The pupa looks dry and lifeless, but inside an amazing transformation is taking place.

Before pupating, many caterpillars spin themselves a protective **cocoon** using threads of silk. The sticky silk comes from little nozzles called **spinnerets** located near a caterpillar's mouth. The silk hardens in the air as the caterpillar wraps itself up. Inside the cocoon the caterpillar molts to become a pupa.

Transformation

It is often possible to see the outline of the future adult's wings and body on the case of a moth pupa. However, inside the hard case is nothing but a milky liquid! Nearly all of the caterpillar's body has broken down to make a kind of soup. Once it has been broken down, the contents of the caterpillar's body are rebuilt into a moth, as outlined on the pupal case. This incredible process is called **metamorphosis** (MEH-TUH-MOR-FUH-SUS), which means "shape changing" in Greek.

Metamorphosis can take anywhere from a few days to many months. When ready, the adult moth flexes its muscles, and the case splits open. A winged insect emerges! At first the damp, crumpled moth cannot fly, but soon its wings uncurl and dry. It is then ready to take to the air. The moth has now reached the final stage in its life cycle. It flies off to find a mate and—if female—lay eggs, so the whole process can begin again.

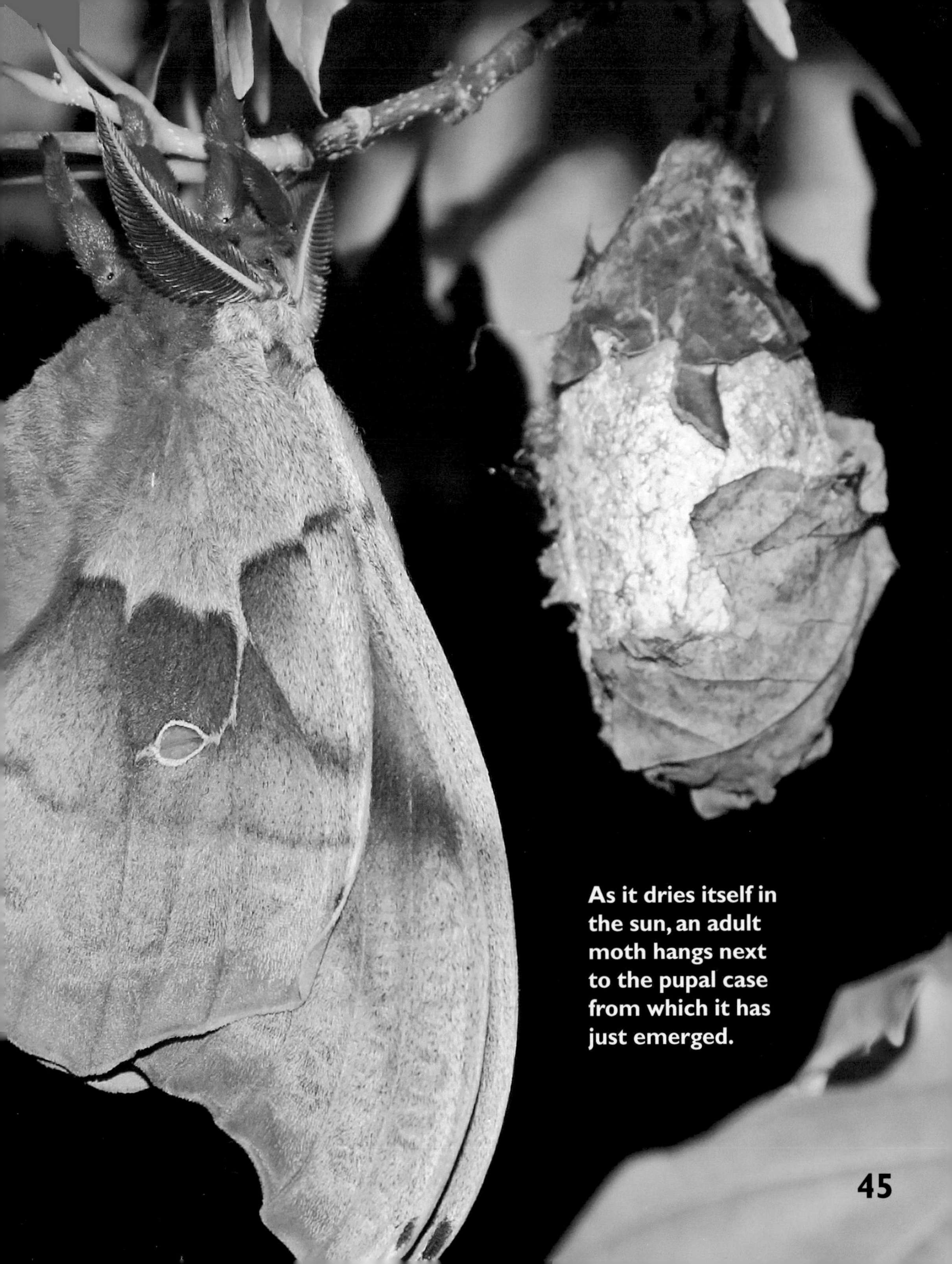

As it dries itself in the sun, an adult moth hangs next to the pupal case from which it has just emerged.

Adult silk moths emerge from their silky cocoons.

Friend or Foe?

Some people view moths as pests. It is true that many moths are destructive, particularly as caterpillars. For example, owlet moth larvae are known as cutworms. They hide underground in the day and eat the leaves of garden plants at night. Clothes moth larvae feed on wool and nibble holes in sweaters and coats.

However, moths are also useful. Moths help gardeners and farmers by pollinating fruit trees, crops, and other flowering plants.

The most important moth is perhaps the silk moth. This insect produces one of the most luxurious of all materials—silk. This amazing fiber is made from the threads that silk moth caterpillars use to weave their cocoons.

Spotting Moths

If you want to find out more about the types of moths that live in your neighborhood you will need a white sheet and a powerful flashlight. Hang the sheet up outside at night and shine the light on it. That will create a bright white area in the darkness that will attract moths and other insects. You could photograph the moths that land on the sheet. Turn the flashlight off when you are done, and the moths will fly away.

Moths also enjoy rotting fruit. Mash some very ripe fruit in a bowl, and add water and a little sugar. Paint the sweet liquid onto a strip of fence in your backyard. The sweet smell will bring the moths flocking. Try to identify the moths you see using a field guide. You will be amazed at the wide variety of moths. Try that at different times of the year as the moth population is always changing. Some moths are active in spring, while others are active in fall.

Words to Know

Antennas An insect's "feelers." Moths use theirs for smelling.

Camouflage The colors and patterns on a body that help it stay hidden in its surroundings.

Caterpillar The second stage in a moth's life, after it hatches from the egg.

Cocoon The protective case around a pupa.

Larva A young insect; a moth larva is known as a caterpillar.

Mate When a male and female animal come together to produce young; also means a breeding partner.

Metamorphosis The process by which an insect changes from larva to adult.

Molting	When a growing animal sheds its skin or hair.
Nectar	A sugary liquid produced by flowers.
Pollen	Powder used in plant breeding.
Predators	Animals that hunt other animals.
Prey	An animal that is eaten by another.
Proboscis	The strawlike feeding tube of a moth.
Pupa	The third stage in a moth's life, before it becomes an adult.
Species	The scientific term for animals of the same type that can breed together.
Spinnerets	Structures near a caterpillar's mouth that produce silk.
Thorax	The middle section of an insect's body, to which the legs and wings attach.

Find Out More

Books

Drits, D. *Silkworm Moths.* Minneapolis, Minnesota: Lerner Publications, 2002.

Kottke, J. *From Caterpillar to Moth.* New York: Children's Press, 2000.

Loewen, N. *Night Fliers: Moths in Your Backyard.* Minneapolis, Minnesota: Picture Window Books, 2004.

Web sites

A Guide to Moths and Butterflies
www.butterfliesandmoths.org
A set of maps, species lists, and images of moths.

Encyclopedia Smithsonia
www.si.edu/Encyclopedia_SI/nmnh/buginfo/moths.htm
Information about moths from all around the world.

Index

A, B, C

abdomen 11,
antennas 8, 18, 19, 20, 23, 35
Atlas moth 27, 38
attraction to light 17, 48
body 8, 11
burnet moth 30
butterflies 5, 7, 8, 9, 11, 12, 24, 25, 31
camouflage 25, 32, 40
catching moths 17, 48
caterpillars 5, 32, 33, 35, 36, 39, 40, 41, 43, 47
clothes moth 47
cocoon 43, 46, 47
color vision 20
compound eyes 20, 21, 35
cutworms 47

D, E, F

death's head hawk moth 42
defense 28, 40
drinking 23
eardrums 19
eating 36, 39, 43
eggs 5, 14, 32, 33, 34, 44
enemies 5, 25, 28, 40
eyesight 19
feet 19, 23
flowers 9, 20, 23, 24
flying 8, 9, 14, 15

G, H, I

geometer moth 35
great tiger moth 25
habitats 12
hair 35, 41
hawk moths 14, 15, 22
hearing 19
hovering 15, 22
inchworm 35
insects 7, 11, 20, 24, 48
Io moth 28, 29

M, N, O

mating 31
metamorphosis 44
migration 15
molting 38, 39, 43
mouthparts 5, 23
nectar 23, 24
oleander hawk moth 15
owlet moth 47

P, S

peppered moth 25
poisons 30, 40
polyphemus moth 37
predators 28, 30, 43
proboscis 22, 23
promethia moth 33
pupa 42, 43, 44, 45
puss moth 37
scales 6, 7
silk moth 46, 47
simple eyes 20, 35
size 11, 27
skin 35, 38, 39
smell 18, 19, 23, 31
species 7, 11, 12, 17
speed 15
spinnerets 43
sycamore moth 41

T, U, W

taste organs 19, 23
thorax 11, 15, 19
tiger moth 25, 28
underwing moth 25
wings 5, 6, 7, 8, 10, 11, 14, 15, 25, 28, 29, 30, 45